For the Love of Dog

For the Love of Dog

Why Man Is Dog's Best Friend

TRACY FORD

*photographs by Bill Jayne
and Stacie Bauerle*

CUMBERLAND HOUSE
NASHVILLE, TENNESSEE

For my mother, Adeline, who always knew. And who taught me to love and respect all of God's creations. And for Bill, who trusted me with his best friend.

—Tracy

For Dusty and Sadie, you taught me about life, love, and letting go. For Joshua, your awe and love for animals shows the sweet spirit within that will carry you through the rest of your life.

—Stacie

For Mom and Dad, who taught me all about how to love a pet. For my wife, who knew just when I needed a dog in the house. For Chris, Heather, Will, Maddie, and Ryan, who show me every day why kids need dogs. And for Buster, whose love will never be forgotten. I miss you, brown dog.

—Bill

ACKNOWLEDGMENTS

We would like to thank Ron Pitkin and Julie Jayne of Cumberland House. We would also like to thank our editor, Lisa Taylor, for bringing our thoughts and images together so well. And, of course, our thanks go out to the real stars of the show: Rizpah, Endora, Buster, Sadie, Holmes, Maggie, Cameron, Shannon, Bailey, Rascal, Kayla, Zeus, Athena, Chopper, Nestle, Chenzia, Chance, Shadow, Sissy, Dixie, Mrs. Peele, Mrs. Howell, and all the others who we know will forgive us for not naming them since they get all the recognition they need from their best friend.

INTRODUCTION

The clicking of toenails on the kitchen floor, the thump of a tail responding to my voice in the dark, the familiar push and grunt of a long stretch as I roll over the first time in the light of morning—these are a few of my favorite things. And since you are reading this, I might assume they are some of yours, too.

My family always had animals when I was growing up. Standard pets such as dogs, cats, birds, and fish passed through our household over the years. We had a fenced-in backyard and took good care of our dogs, but their attitudes reflected being "caged." Our dogs were not allowed in the house—ever. And though they were friendly enough and fun to play with, given the chance they would burst through the gate and run like there was no tomorrow. As a child I wondered why a creature would want to run away from his family, from the very ones, perhaps the only ones, who would love and care for him.

I was thrilled when, at the age of twelve, I got my own dog. *My* dog. Not only was she my first dog, she was also our first small dog and the first allowed to live in the house. She was my responsibility and it was understood that if I trained her and picked up after her she was welcome to become a part of our household. She was a "Pek-a-poo," part Pekingese and part poodle. My uncle had a poodle, so we all knew how smart that half would be, and the Pekingese seemed to add a touch of humility.

My new puppy was sweet, smart, and quiet. She learned quickly and devoted herself to pleasing me. We were inseparable. At first, she slept in a box next to my bed. After spending a couple of nights trying to sleep with one arm hanging off my bed into her box I decided something had to change. Since she already went through the night without a bathroom break, it proved too easy to lift the tiny thing up onto the bed with me. Later, when I learned that allowing a dog to share your bed may confuse your dog with regard to pack hierarchy, it was too late. And frankly, I don't know whether that knowledge would have stopped me. My personal opinion on this topic is that it should be decided on a dog-by-dog basis. I have been fortunate that none of my dogs have ever questioned who is in charge.

With the exception of the boxer mix that currently shares my home with me, *the* dog in my life was a ten-pound blonde puff named Rizpah, or "Riz" to her friends. Riz cared only for me. She was happy to see any of the family come home, happy to jump in their lap for a minute of petting, but even then her eyes were on me. I could wink at her from across the room and she would run and jump into my arms. If I left the room, Riz followed. If a door closed behind me, Riz sat at that door until I came back through it. She was happiest comfortably straddling my forearm, for she fit perfectly between the crook of my elbow and the palm of my hand. All her years, she flatly refused to walk in front of me, but was never more than three steps behind. She had to keep me in sight. The only unfortunate thing about Riz was that when I wasn't around she could be difficult to deal with. It was as if she suddenly went dumb and forgot everything she had ever been taught. I never intended that sort of dependence; it just happened.

Rizpah lived well into her seventeenth year. When the time came, I said goodbye to her. I hugged her one last time. Squeezed her tight. I like to think she knew it, and thought it felt as wonderful as I did.

The news that Riz was gone traveled fast, and shortly afterward I began receiving certificates of money donated in Rizpah's name to worthy causes, cards bearing warm words of sympathy, and many beautiful flowers. Before long I had to dedicate a table to display all of these things, and as I arranged them I was hit with a greater understanding of how much I had lost. You see, except for my family, Riz had been in my life longer than anyone. I was thirty-six years old, and I had just lost my oldest, dearest, and most trusted companion. As I stepped back and looked at the flowers and cards on the table before me, I realized my friends already knew that.

I now know why the dogs of my early childhood tried to run away. I believe they did not feel like part of the family. They were dogs separated from their pack. After all, if they were part of our pack they would not eat, sleep, and spend most of their waking hours alone, staring at the world through the crossed wires of a chain-link fence.

Dogs find freedom in belonging. They need a family and they need to know where they fit in with that family—their pack. In my years of living and working with dogs, I have formed the opinion that if you own a dog you must commit to bringing the dog *into your life*. That is how you learn about each other. My dog would spend every minute of every day on my pillow in my bed if she could. She has a pet door and is free to roam the backyard and chase squirrels or dig up irises, but she waits. She waits until the rest of her family gets home to eat, drink, and play—and later meet her back in the bed again.

Years ago my mother said, "I never worry about my kids getting into trouble or not fitting in. I've watched each of you worry and fuss over animals all your lives. It shows you have compassion and you know what is fair and right when it comes to how to treat others." Perhaps that is why, as a child, after collecting a mason jar full of lightning bugs, I insisted on releasing them. Or after watching as my father carefully tied a piece of thread on the leg of a June bug, then "flying" it around for a while, I demanded that the thread be removed from the insect's leg. I wanted it untied and removed completely, but had to settle for it being cut. My father assured me that the tiny piece of trailing thread would not impede the day-to-day functions of the June bug. My lingering skepticism over that fact proved to be the end of my June bug–flying days.

I am a dog lover. Truthfully, I am a lover of all animals because they are honest in their representation of themselves. It is something they do without thought and something too few people think of doing at all. I trust dogs. Through any bad time in my life I have had a wonderful, warm companion who seemed to want nothing more than to make me feel better.

The observations and photographs that follow are an effort to share just a few of the hundreds of reasons that we can't get enough of muddy feet, dripping mustaches, persistent barking, and prodding cold noses. Why do we do it? Since you are holding this book, chances are you already know . . . for the love of dog.

For the Love of Dog

he's got my back.

WE'RE BEST FRIENDS BECAUSE

even amid confusion, he never lets me down.

WE'RE BEST FRIENDS BECAUSE

we both sleep well at night knowing there is no limit
to what we would do for each other.

we don't mind cleaning up after each other.

I take notice when she has a good hair day.

WE'RE BEST FRIENDS BECAUSE

she doesn't hesitate to walk into a dark
house in front of me.

WE'RE BEST FRIENDS BECAUSE...

we can keep the same pace for hours.

she can pick me out of a crowd.

WE'RE BEST FRIENDS BECAUSE

she doesn't care if I have morning breath.

WE'RE BEST FRIENDS BECAUSE

she shows me the forest, as well as
the trees . . . one at a time.

she waits for me no matter how late I am.

we see eye to eye.

WE'RE BEST FRIENDS BECAUSE

he senses when I am sad and comforts me.

our contours complement.

it's all good.

WE'RE BEST FRIENDS BECAUSE

he misses me when I'm gone.

our friendship grows stronger as the years go by.

WE'RE BEST FRIENDS BECAUSE...

she just *loves* my truck.

WE'RE BEST FRIENDS BECAUSE

she doesn't embarrass me in public . . . too often.

WE'RE BEST FRIENDS BECAUSE

he works hard, and for the right reasons,
even if only he knows what they are.

WE'RE BEST FRIENDS BECAUSE...

she'll never know the comfort she has given me
and will never ask anything in return.

neither of us wants anyone else around
when the fur starts to fly.

WE'RE BEST FRIENDS BECAUSE

with us, out of sight never means out of mind.

we decided to be the first time we met.

she's the best thing under my tree.

WE'RE BEST FRIENDS BECAUSE

she knows the difference between food and friend.

WE'RE BEST FRIENDS BECAUSE

we can snuggle all we want without it
threatening our friendship.

WE'RE BEST FRIENDS BECAUSE...

all I have to do is ask, and I get his full attention.

he stands his ground—and mine, too, if I need him.

WE'RE BEST FRIENDS BECAUSE

we can read each other like a book—without
telling everything we know.

WE'RE BEST FRIENDS BECAUSE

we have a secret handshake.

WE'RE BEST FRIENDS BECAUSE...

we know how to help each other relax.

it doesn't matter where we're going, but that we're going together.

WE'RE BEST FRIENDS BECAUSE

he shows me it's possible to hold your head high,
even when your tail's dragging.

WE'RE BEST FRIENDS BECAUSE. . .

we help each other start each day
on the right foot and paw.

WE'RE BEST FRIENDS BECAUSE. . .

she always saves me a seat.

WE'RE BEST FRIENDS BECAUSE

she understands when I'm watching the game.

we make each other laugh.

I can always count on her to let me sleep in.

WE'RE BEST FRIENDS BECAUSE

she lives by a beauty-is-where-you-see-it
and freedom-is-where-you-find-it philosophy.

WE'RE BEST FRIENDS BECAUSE

she knows she's *my* Best in Show.

WE'RE BEST FRIENDS BECAUSE. . .

paradise isn't always just over the next hill, but
she'll run and check it out just in case.

she's never a backseat driver.

WE'RE BEST FRIENDS BECAUSE

no matter how long it's been, or what the last
thing I said to her was, she is always
happy to see me again.

any friend of mine is a friend of hers—and if not,
I look twice at my friend.

WE'RE BEST FRIENDS BECAUSE...

he's a foot warmer, a pillow, an armrest, and a security blanket all in one.

WE'RE BEST FRIENDS BECAUSE

I can trust him to keep my secrets.

WE'RE BEST FRIENDS BECAUSE...

he knows when to follow.

WE'RE BEST FRIENDS BECAUSE...

he knows when to get out of the way.

WE'RE BEST FRIENDS BECAUSE

he's shown me how silly it is to be self-conscious.

WE'RE BEST FRIENDS BECAUSE

she plays fair.

WE'RE BEST FRIENDS BECAUSE...

I love her face.

he keeps his schedule flexible for me.

WE'RE BEST FRIENDS BECAUSE

we know each other well enough to know
that we still have more to learn.

WE'RE BEST FRIENDS BECAUSE

she knows just how far she can push me.

WE'RE BEST FRIENDS BECAUSE. . .

we've both been known to sun worship
from time to time.

I can be honest with her about her accessories.

WE'RE BEST FRIENDS BECAUSE

he shows me the same old things in brand new ways.

WE'RE BEST FRIENDS BECAUSE...

he never tires of the old "pull up a stool" joke.

we make sure that good times always follow bad.

WE'RE BEST FRIENDS BECAUSE

she keeps me young by proving we are never
too old to learn new tricks.

WE'RE BEST FRIENDS BECAUSE

she always stands by my side.

WE'RE BEST FRIENDS BECAUSE. . .

she's my only dependable workout partner.

she's not one to carry a grudge.

WE'RE BEST FRIENDS BECAUSE

we compete over which of us worries
more about the other.

WE'RE BEST FRIENDS BECAUSE. . .

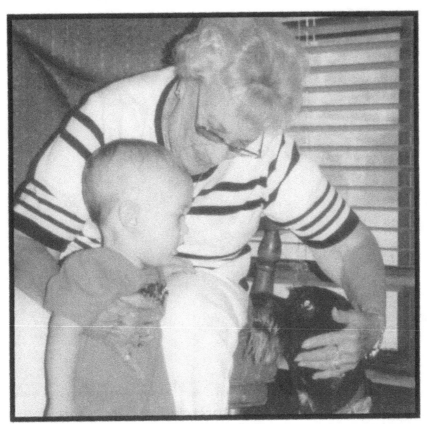

we both know good things come in small packages.

WE'RE BEST FRIENDS BECAUSE...

she taught me that the worst times can be the
best time for friendship.

WE'RE BEST FRIENDS BECAUSE

after all these years she still offers me
a challenge from time to time.

WE'RE BEST FRIENDS BECAUSE

no one else gets away with nudging me
the way he does.

WE'RE BEST FRIENDS BECAUSE...

he is the best, most dependable,
cheapest baby sitter ever.

WE'RE BEST FRIENDS BECAUSE...

her enthusiasm is legendary.

WE'RE BEST FRIENDS BECAUSE

our favorite pastime is spending
time with each other.

WE'RE BEST FRIENDS BECAUSE

she teaches me patience.

I show her patience.

I know his bark is worse than his bite, but I
don't tell the cat.

WE'RE BEST FRIENDS BECAUSE

one way or another we manage to join in
each other's celebrations.

WE'RE BEST FRIENDS BECAUSE

jealousy where she is concerned is natural,
honest, and soon forgotten.

we accept responsibility for each other.

WE'RE BEST FRIENDS BECAUSE...

he wouldn't have it any other way.

WE'RE BEST FRIENDS BECAUSE

we suffer no language barriers.

WE'RE BEST FRIENDS BECAUSE

she knows I would do anything for her—
and sometimes expects it.

WE'RE BEST FRIENDS BECAUSE...

I know what's for her own good.

WE'RE BEST FRIENDS BECAUSE...

she's always up for a nap.

WE'RE BEST FRIENDS BECAUSE

she wants nothing more than I have to give
and gives nothing less than I need.

WE'RE BEST FRIENDS BECAUSE

she helps me see life's little problems as little.

WE'RE BEST FRIENDS BECAUSE...

she has no idea how gorgeous she is.

he is fearless in his protection of our home.

WE'RE BEST FRIENDS BECAUSE

no fence will ever come between us.

WE'RE BEST FRIENDS BECAUSE

we both appreciate life's simple pleasures.

WE'RE BEST FRIENDS BECAUSE...

her presence soothes my frayed nerves.

WE'RE BEST FRIENDS BECAUSE...

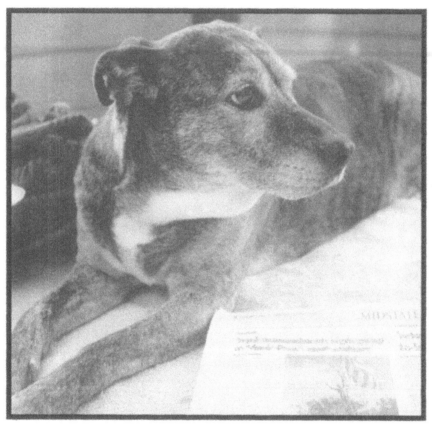

she politely lies *next* to my newspaper, not on it.

WE'RE BEST FRIENDS BECAUSE

when life is crazy, a few soft words and a quiet
moment are all we really need.

WE'RE BEST FRIENDS BECAUSE

he can always find a good time
somewhere in my bad mood.

WE'RE BEST FRIENDS BECAUSE...

we both know when it's time for the short leash.

we'll always need each other.

WE'RE BEST FRIENDS BECAUSE

it's nice to know that you are someone's priority.

WE'RE BEST FRIENDS BECAUSE

he'd never mislead me.

WE'RE BEST FRIENDS BECAUSE...

we're both pups at heart.

WE'RE BEST FRIENDS BECAUSE...

whenever I need her, all I do is call.

WE'RE BEST FRIENDS BECAUSE

we weather the storm together.

WE'RE BEST FRIENDS BECAUSE...

we share the same memories.